Leafy and Sprucy

Kenneth David Brubacher

AuthorHouse™
1663 Liberty Drive
Bloomington, IN 47403
www.authorhouse.com
Phone: 1 (800) 839-8640

Published by AuthorHouse 12/10/2015

ISBN: 978-1-5049-6697-9 (sc)
ISBN: 978-1-5049-6699-3 (hc)
ISBN: 978-1-5049-6698-6 (e)

Library of Congress Control Number: 2015920461

Print information available on the last page.

This book is printed on acid-free paper.

Illustrations by Eric Smith / IronMedia.ca Printed by St. Jacobs Printery Ltd.,
St. Jacobs, ON Bound by Lehman Bookbinding Ltd., Kitchener, ON

A Hat & Hammer Production
A Division of Brubacher Technologies Ltd.
Visit: hat@hammerproductions.com

Made in Canada

authorHOUSE®

Fly

The Watcher

The Poor Shoemaker

Mennonite Cobbler

There's An Angel Under My Bed

Commotion in the Manure Yard

Fire Dragon Moon

The Book of Truth and Wisdom

Amos and Salina Go To Town

Dedicated to

Julia Lily Hiller

My Granddaughter

She of Many Smiles

Good morning Sprucy.

And a Very Good Morning to you as well, Leafy.
You are looking particularly beautiful these days, what with your wonderful red and yellow leaves.

Why, thank you, Sprucy! That is very lovely thing for you to say. You always look wonderful, always the same no matter where we are in the Circle of the Sun. Rain, shine, or snow – always gorgeous! And soon especially gorgeous when they come and do circles of string all around you, so that when it gets dark all the little jars attached to the strings wake up the glow worms and fireflies inside. Very Beautiful!

It looks like it's going to be another very fine day - a Goldilocks Day - not too hot and not too cold; just right! You are now very tall and your arms almost touch mine. You have grown a great deal since I was brought here.

Yes, that is true. I remember very well the day you came. Men had dug a hole in the ground on the other side of StoneMan where you now stand. You were not quite as tall as StoneMan and had a brown bag tied around your roots. They stood you up in the hole and filled in around your roots with earth taken from the hole. Then they gently packed the ground around your base and gave you a drink. They were quite careful and I was glad to have you here with me. And I still am! It is very pleasant to have a companion with whom to have conversation.

Indeed it is. I was only coming awake then and have grown much since. Not as tall as you, Leafy, but still very much taller than back then. Do you remember what it was like for you when you came awake?

Oh yes, I do. Not perfectly, you understand; things were a bit fuzzy at first, but soon I was wide awake. It was right here where I now stand and the snows were starting to go away. One by one the days got warmer and the bright yellow ball in the sky, what we now know to call Sun, was showing its face longer each day. I was all alone then because all the other trees were far enough down the block that I could not hear what they were talking about, or for me to speak with them, so I had to learn about things perhaps slower than if I were closer to them.

It appeared that I was in a place where something special was going to happen because the people spoke of a thing called The War and what they were going to do here When The War Is Over.

Sure enough, a few Circles of the Sun after I woke up, men came and dug a big hole and then brought StoneMan and set him up on the many small stones they put first into the bottom of the hole. Then they carved names into the rock base on which StoneMan stands. I know they are names because each time they offer WorthShip somebody stands in front of StoneMan, looks at the markings and slowly calls them, as though they might appear. Perhaps they are the departed priests of their religion, for they are held in great reverence. Many people, a large number dressed very much like StoneMan, stand in silence with far away looks, and put flowers in the little garden they made at the base of the large rock on which he stands.

This was a fair number of snows before you came. I was all alone then, with nobody for conversation. It was also the time in the Circle of the Sun when my leaves had just fallen off.

I have also often wondered exactly what StoneMan is, or what he represents.

I think he must be a god. They call that stick he carries Gun. It must be a magic wand or a talisman of great power. Every Circle of the Sun, when the snows are soon coming, people come and offer WorthShip here at the shrine of their god StoneMan. I think he must be a relative to the gods to which they offer WorthShip in Reena across the street. I remember when they built Reena. They said many times We need a Reena. So they built a Reena which I am pretty sure is a temple where they give WorthShip to the religion called Hockey. It is a Hockey Reena.

Yes, said Sprucy, that is probably true. There is no question that the building across the street must be a temple of some kind. They say We will have Hockey in a Reena, so this must indeed be a temple Reena. I remember well when they did this. It was in the days when pretty much everybody had stopped going by in buggies and wagons pulled by the horses who Do the Clip-Clop. They were now driving cars and trucks, and it was the men in trucks who brought the materials from which they built Reena. All except the people in black hats and coats and black buggies. They never stopped to help build Reena. And they never changed. They have always driven past being pulled by their horses who Do the Clip-Clop.

Now, many times each day, cars park over there, and out of them come many people with strange-looking very colorful clothing, including big bulky short pants. At first they did this only when it was cold with snow, but now they do it all the time, even when it is hot outside.

They all go into Reena carrying high boots with shiny runners on the bottom and a strange stick with a sort of angled hook on one end. They always refer to it as Hockey Stick. I can see it is a stick, so the religion must be called Hockey.

Yes, said Sprucy, I think that is true. Also their religion must require a lot of energy because they all go running in. And then later, after they offer their WorthShip, they come out again but are moving much more slowly. I am not sure what all those inside Reena do in the practise of the religion Hockey, but when they come back out again they speak with great reverence regarding the gods of Hockey. For example the god SlapShot. And ShutOut.

Also other deities which they call HighSticking and BodyCheck. BodyCheck must be some sort of cleansing ritual performed before they can be found worthy to salute the Hockey gods with a ceremonial HighSticking. It all must be a very strenuous matter done with much religious fervor.

True, said Leafy. The people who give WorthShip to the religion Hockey in Reena are mostly much younger than those who offer WorthShip to the god StoneMan, therefore the religion Hockey must be relatively new. Also over in Reena, if it is not too noisy on the street, we can hear them sing. Mostly it is the same hymn to their faith: " Oh Canada, our home and native land..." after which they perform the ritual called MuchNoise. Pretty sure the gods of Hockey require sacrifice involving MuchNoise, including the sacraments Yelling and Screaming, and the creating of a powerful high-pitched sound like the rushing of a mighty wind through one of my knot-holes on a very windy night.

Yes. I think you are probably right. And I know it is a talisman called Hockey Stick that they take in there because one person asked another after the WorthShip service was over Where is your Hockey Stick? And the other fellow said I broke it on a SlapShot. Well, Hockey Stick had looked plenty strong to me, therefore the god SlapShot must be very tough and very hard as well, if the man giving WorthShip broke his stick over a SlapShot.

Yes, said Leafy, I agree. That is most likely the case. Perhaps our god here StoneMan is related to the gods of Hockey. After all, Hockey Stick looks a lot like the stick they call gun StoneMan carries at his side.

And also I wonder why he puts his hand up above his eye. It must represent some ritual that the god StoneMan finds to be a sign of respect, commanding this ritual that happens once every Circle of the Sun along about when it looks like the snows will soon come. At first I thought I might be dreaming this because it always happens when it is starting to get cold and I am growing sleepy. But sometimes it is still quite warm and I know I am not yet that drowsy. Many of the people who then come to offer WorthShip wear clothes in the same manner as StoneMan, and also put one hand up to their eye. I think the religion where they offer WorthShip to the god StoneMan is an older religion. Most of the people who come to give WorthShip to StoneMan are older, some quite old indeed. And each Circle of the Sun there are fewer and fewer of them. Here at the rituals to StoneMan they sing different songs and then stand silently after one of the men dressed like StoneMan makes silvery music.

Yes, said Sprucy, it is very peculiar, but it must be a part of their religion to do this. It is interesting that they have religious services nearly all day every day in Reena across the street, but they only come in reverence to the god StoneMan once each Circle of the Sun, when your leaves fall off. Very strange.

Strange indeed, said Leafy, but not nearly as strange as those who offer WorthShip in the religion whose deities are the gods PickUp. There appear to be quite a few different flavors of the gods PickUp, including ShinyNew, LoudThroaty, and ReallyJacked. They stop on the side of the street outside Reena and hold a communion service which seems to center around the ritual sacrament called Buddy Have a Beer. Many of the followers of the religion PickUp also give WorthShip in the temple Rena.

This is true, said Sprucy. Also the gods PickUp can run very fast. I well remember the night when a god PickUp came up the street very, very fast and ran into your body. It was a terrible thing! The god PickUp was badly wrinkled and out of it came dancing tongues of light which were very hot and climbed up onto some of your arms. It was awful!

Yes, said Leafy. The dancing tongues of light were so hot that they started to make several of my arms go black and actually consumed some of my fingers and leaves. It hurt very much indeed. I did not know what to do. But then a big red house on wheels making much noise came up the street. Men in red hats and yellow coats rushed out of it. Then they dragged a big snake out of their red house on wheels.

They pulled a knot out of the side of that little red stump over there and made the snake bite down hard on the knot-hole. Clearly the snake had been trained to suck large amounts of magic rain out of the little red stump, and then they took the other end of this snake and sprayed this rain onto the dancing tongues of hot light. Yes, it was a terrible thing indeed. And it hurt. But thankfully the dancing tongues went away.

Yes, said Sprucy. I have no doubt that it hurt a lot. I felt very sorry for you. One of the men in a red hat said that the man in the god PickUp had too much Beer. Perhaps he had been offering WorthShip at another place of congregation for the gods PickUp, and had partaken of the ritual Buddy Have A Beer with too much religious fervor.

Yes, Sprucy, standing here is not without danger.

Yet even so I like it here. The summers are best. People come and sit at the tables under my arms in the shade, away from the heat of the day, and take things out of their baskets to eat and to drink. This is very pleasant indeed, and makes the cold and snow worthwhile. Then, later in the evenings, the young people come and sit, and sometimes take a sharp tool and make markings in my skin. It tickles. It seems to make them happy too, because they often giggle and coo like the pigeons which perch on my arms. Perhaps they think that I am a god too, and this is their Way of WorthShip. They mostly sit very closely together and say strange things in soft voices. And though my hearing is very good, I many times cannot hear what they are saying.

Yes, said Sprucy, I have often seen this. However, I am not so sure that what they have to say has very much to do with either intelligence, WorthShip, or anything beyond their own mutual edification. But it clearly makes them happy, so what harm there.

I have for many long years wondered about the strange-looking stick called Gun that StoneMan is carrying. Each time the old people come to give WorthShip they bring with them men who are dressed much like StoneMan, and who also carry sticks very like that which StoneMan holds.

Consider that from time to time a man in a god PickUp gets out and points a stick similar to what the god StoneMan holds, and points it into my arms high up. Then a loud noise comes out of the stick called Gun and a large bird falls down off my arm and lies still. Is this a sacrifice to me, the god Leafy? Or is this a different PickUp ritual called Good Shot? Because they then say Buddy Have A Beer to mark their WorthShip.

I have often wondered exactly why they brought us here, said Sprucy. Perhaps we were brought here to keep watch over StoneMan. Or maybe we are gods too. After all, the people start coming past when they are very young and then get older and older. Then they seem to go away and not come back anymore, right about when the long black strange-looking car goes by, followed by many other cars going very slowly. So the people come and go - and we stay. After all, you were here before the god StoneMan. Does that make you a god too?

I am not sure, but if I am a god then you also, Sprucy, must be a god. Every year when I am nearly asleep the people come and wind much string with tiny glass jars around you and put a star on top. Then at night they cause glow worms and fireflies to dance with much color inside the jars, while they sing wonderful songs to you. Yes, I think you, at least, are a god. Or maybe we are of the lesser gods and are here to offer WorthShip to those gods who are greater, such as Sun and Rain, who were here before we came. After all, we could not have life without them.

But one matter of WorthShip has always been a mystery to me. It has to do with the People with Black Hats pulled by horses that still Do The Clip-Clop. Perhaps this is an ancient rhythmic dance. I have watched them for very many Circles of the Sun and they have never changed. Everybody else has changed, including their clothes and their cars and trucks. All changed many times. But the Black Hats who Do The Clip-Clop have always stayed exactly the same.

I could never figure out their religion. They never offered WorthShip to the gods SlapShot or ShutOut in the temple Reena. They never stopped nor took off their hats at the Shrine to the god StoneMan. They always went on by exactly as they always did, and with their Sunday Faces firmly pasted on.

But now I think I know. I am not sure if they have forsaken their old gods, but they now for sure offer WorthShip to the new gods. The gods of the Shining Faces. The god BlackBerry and the god SmartPhone, just like most other people going by. They have silent communion with their new gods using only their fingers, and they can do this even while their horses Do the Clip-Clop. Yet their hats and faces never change.

Yes. You are right. Perhaps there has been a conference of the gods, and there has been merger or an acquisition. But certainly the new gods of the Shining Faces are the most powerful I have ever seen. After all, do we not now see even the Black Hats offer WorthShip to these new gods, while also eating and drinking things that until now we saw only consumed by the people who offer WorthShip in Reena and PickUp? Things like the dark liquid from the glass jar god named Coke, and his servants Crunchy Things in Crinkly Bags??

About the Author

Kenneth David Brubacher was born into a large family of sort of Mennonites in Elmira, ON, through no fault of his own. He was encouraged to make an attempt at becoming a normal human being, but clearly with limited success. To the surprise of nearly everyone he graduated from secondary school in 1970.

From there he traveled the world extensively, turning his hand to many kinds of jobs, and eventually returned to Elmira having accomplished very little. He got work as a millwright, but it was soon evident that he was a millwrong. After being mercifully fired from that job he went trucking and almost immediately distinguished himself (Summa Cum Laude with Oak Leaf Cluster and Silver Star) by destroying the truck.

He married and begat two lovely daughters who took after their mother in many wonderful ways, and turned out normal. It was considered a blessing that he had no sons because there was a high degree of probability that they might well grow up to be like their dad.

Knowing little about shoes, and even less about feet, he then took over his father's shoe repair shop and started to make shoes by hand along about April Fools' Day 1978. Very few people caught on. It was obvious that people whose feet were so bad that they sought out the services of a cobbler were not very fussy. The business prospered in spite of its inherent inadequacies.

He also applied himself to many varieties of sport, establishing a universal mediocrity in their pursuit seldom seen. When his body was sufficiently trashed he took up umpiring baseball, where it was observed that his training must have occurred under the tender administrations of the CNIB.

Currently he makes his home on a rented farm near Creemore, ON, and repairs a few shoes in his small shop in Collingwood. The farmhouse will soon become a gravel pit, whereupon it was his intent to establish institutions where Mennonites could go to seek quiet enjoyment. This, of course, until it was pointed out to him that they had already done it. These establishments are known as Mennonite Farms.

The author heartily recommends that any reader who takes a notion to write and produce a book or a play, then to lie down on the couch and watch videos of fawns gamboling in a sun-splashed meadow full of butterflies - until the feeling goes away.

It is hoped that you enjoy the book, and that its contents and presentation may provide therapeutic assistance in the remedy of your insomnia.

Printed in the United States
By Bookmasters